# Major Incident Management for IT Operat

## By Christopher Skelton

This book is dedicated to my ever patient and loving family:

Estelle, Connor and Elysia.

## Preface

There are numerous books on incident management from different best practices, but few that provide a comprehensive guide to major incident management for information technology IT. The ITIL® IT Operations Manual has 3 paragraphs dedicated to major incident management. Major incident management has become a career choice as many businesses employ specialists responsible for returning services to normal as soon as possible after a major incident while minimising impact to the business. Hence, this book has been written focusing on those elements of major incident management which were not covered in this level of detail by best practice frameworks or by other authors. This book has been written considering the challenges faced by major incident managers focusing on the definition and establishment of a major incident management process, roles and responsibilities, skills, showing value through matrices and self-management during a major incident.

This book takes the reader through all aspects of major incident management:

**1. Introduction to Major Incident Management** – A high level introduction discussing what a major incident is and what major incident management is and is not.

**2. Defining What Constitutes a Major Incident** – Rules for assigning priorities to Incidents, including the definition of what constitutes a major incident as agreed between IT and the business. It outlines sequential steps which could help define which incidents should trigger the invocation of the major incident process.

**3. Define Interfaces with Other Functions** – Defines the relationship with all stakeholders, building the cross-functional team.

**4. Define the Engagement and Escalation Plan** – Processes that need to be in place to ensure rapid engagement when a major incident is reported.

**5. Major Incident Management Tools and Infrastructure** – These will enable efficient, effective and rapid resolution of major incidents.

**6. Define the Major Incident Management Process** – The sequence of steps that should occur following a major incident being reported. This includes process flow charts and the definition of roles and responsibilities.

**7. Roles and Responsibilities** – Agreed and defined responsibilities for all of the cross-functional major incident management team members.

**8. Communication Plan** – Defined and agreed plan to communicate a major incidents status across all stakeholders,

**9. Post Major Incident Review** – Identify lessons learnt to enable continuous service improvement and handover to problem management.

**10. SLA's, OLA's and UC's** – Defining and agreeing the major incident management service level agreements with the business and the operating level agreements and third party underpinning contracts required to support these agreements.

**11. Major Incident Management Matrix** – Measuring performance against service level agreements and key performance indicators.

**12. Major Incident Manager Self-Management** – Tips and tricks for the major incident manager to manage the incident as effectively and efficiently as possible in stressful scenarios.

# Table of Contents

# 1 Introduction

In this section major incident management will be defined at a fundamental level. It explains the principles of classifying an incident as a major incident and major incident management's place in the incident management lifecycle.

## 1.1 What is a Major Incident?

Before defining a major incident we need to define an incident. ITIL defines an incident as:

*"An unplanned interruption to an IT Service or reduction in the quality of an IT service".*

This definition encompasses all IT incidents irrespective if severity. To define a major incident is more difficult as "major" is subjective. ITIL defines a major incident as:

*"The highest category of impact for an Incident. A major Incident results in significant disruption to the business".*

So how much disruption is required before it is considered to be a major incident? **The answer is simply that the business and IT agree what constitutes a major incident.** We would typically know an IT major incident when we see it. Examples could be a high number of impacted users or depriving the business on one or more crucial services. With different service level agreement (SLA) parameters across businesses/organisations each will decide which priority incidents will be categorised as major incidents to meet their unique requirements. This is usually defined by an agreed impact/urgency matrix. Incident classification will be explained in more detail in section 2.

Another definition to be aware of is a "crisis". A crisis is a major incident but with the added element of being a threat to the organisation as a whole. An example could be a catastrophic and persistent network outage impacting the entire organisations ability to function.

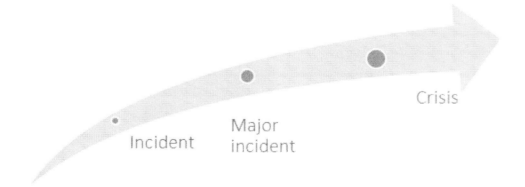

*Figure 1: Focus on major incident.*

## 1.2 What is Major Incident Management?

The purpose of the incident management process is to restore normal service operation as quickly as possible and minimize the adverse impact on business operations, ensuring that agreed levels of service quality are maintained. If an event has significant impact or urgency for the business/organisation it demands a response beyond the routine incident management process. When an incident is defined as a major incident normal incident management procedures are abandoned and major incident management procedures are invoked. Major incident management procedures have an emphasis on urgent response, communications with all stakeholders, resource engagement, deployment and coordination.

A major incident procedure should establish a dedicated major incident team led by a major incident manager. This team will concentrate on the incident alone and ensure that adequate resources are provided to finding a resolution as quickly as possible. Major incident management may differ from crisis management in that a crisis requires a response beyond the routine major incident management process. This would include strategic issues such as managing media relations and shareholder confidence, and when to invoke business continuity plans. Large complex organisations will have a crisis management strategy, model and plan that augments major incident management. In other organisations the major incident process will suffice. The quantifiable differences between a crisis and a major incident in large complex organisations is the scope of impact and complexity.

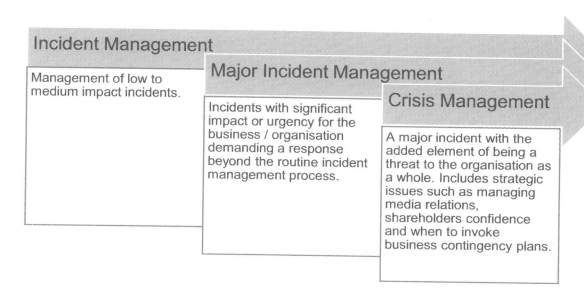

*Figure 2: The overlap between incident management, major incident management and crisis management.*

## 1.3 What Major Incident Management is not

Major incident management focuses only on the subset of incidents defined as "major". **What constitutes a major incident is agreed between the business and IT.** It is not problem management, it is not root cause analysis, it is not change management and it is not finding a permanent solution. These are all separate processes. Incident management is about restoring services as quickly as possible which may include a temporary workaround. Major incident management has the same objective as incident management but the skillsets are different.

# 2 Defining What Constitutes a Major Incident

Rules need to be defined for assigning priorities to Incidents, including the definition of what constitutes a major incident. The following sequential steps could help define which incidents should trigger the invocation of the major incident process.

*Figure 3: Steps to define what constitutes a major incident*

## 2.1 Review of Service Level Agreements and Service Catalogues

Working with the Business Relationship Manager and business representatives determine the mission critical services and components. This will define which services, when impacted by an incident, could invoke the major incident management process. One of the ways to do this would be to categorise services based on their criticality:

| Service Category | A | B | C | D |
|---|---|---|---|---|
| Applicability | Vital business functions / Core shared infrastructure | Important Business functions / Vital support functions | Medium production systems | Occasional use or low priority support systems |
| Criticality | Mission Critical | Critical | Important | Low |
| Service Availability Service Level Agreement | Business – 99% Infrastructure – 99.5% | 99% | 98.5% | 95% |

*Table 1: Service categories*

This is a first pass on defining which categories of services may require the major incident management procedure to be invoked for high severity incidents. This can initially be drafted by holding brainstorming sessions among the relevant support groups, service desk supervisors, incident and problem managers and business representatives. These sessions can be repeated on periodic review to ensure that they remain relevant. In this example IT and the business may agree that category C and D incidents could not by definition of their criticality be of a severity that would invoke a major incident management process.

The organisation may have subcategories. There may be a select few services in category A that are as marked as "franchise risk" (or any other appropriate name). Examples of these services could be the primary customer facing front end system of a corporate bank used to initiate all transactions or an airports core system that receives and routes flight information and schedules. Any disruption of these services would have the severest of impacts to the business.

This is a useful exercise before defining incident priorities as it limits the justifiable invocation of the major incident management process to the critical services.

## 2.2 Define Categories of Urgency

The definitions of categories of urgency will be unique to each organisation. Each organisation will have multiple urgency scenarios. The following table provides some examples of one potential urgency scenario by organisation type. When determining an incident's urgency the highest relevant category is chosen:

| Category | Urgency Scenario Description |
| --- | --- |
| High | Financial bank: Highly time sensitive transaction processing cannot be completed<br>Airport: IT baggage transfer application failure with flight due to depart within the next 2 hours at risk of cancellation.<br>Internet service provider: Significant number of customers have lost their internet connectivity.<br>Any: Systems have been hacked or infected by a virus impacting multiple users with a risk of spreading. |
| Medium | Financial bank: Transaction processing delayed with country clearing house cut off 8 or more hours away.<br>Airport: IT baggage transfer application degraded performance with flight due to depart in more than 2 but less than 8 hours away at risk of cancellation. |
| Low | Financial bank: System providing monthly volume reports to the central bank failing with report delivery deadline 1 week away.<br>Airport: Degraded performance of baggage transfer application with some passengers booked on flights at risk of having their baggage delivered on a later flight. |

*Table 2: Categories of urgency*

## 2.3 Define Categories of Impact

As with urgency, the definitions of categories of impact will be unique to each organisation. The following table provides some examples of one potential impact scenario by organisation type. When determining an incident's impact, the highest relevant category is chosen:

| Category | Impact Scenario Description |
| --- | --- |
| High | Financial bank: Value of transactions missing clearing cut off exceeds £1,000,000.<br>Airport: Flights cancelled or delayed by more than 1 hour. |

| Category | Impact Scenario Description |
|---|---|
|  | Internet service provider: Significant number of customers have lost their internet connectivity. Any: Systems have been hacked or infected by a virus impacting multiple users preventing or contaminating highly time sensitive work and data security at risk. |
| Medium | Financial bank: Value of transactions missing clearing cut off exceeds $100 000 but is less than $1,000,000. Airport: Flights delayed by under one hour. |
| Low | Financial bank: Value of transactions missing clearing cut off is less than $100 000. Airport: Only a few passengers had their baggage delivered on later flights. |

Table 3: Categories of impact

## 2.4 Define Priority Classes

Incident priority is derived from urgency and impact by an incident priority matrix:

| | | Impact | | |
|---|---|---|---|---|
| | | High | Medium | Low |
| **Urgency** | High | Priority 1 | Priority 2 | Priority 3 |
| | Medium | Priority 2 | Priority 3 | Priority 4 |
| | Low | Priority 3 | Priority 4 | Priority 5 |

Table 4: Incident priority matrix

Now in agreement with the business target response time and target resolution times can be defined for each priority class:

| Priority | Description | Target Response Time | Target Resolution Time |
|---|---|---|---|
| Priority 1 | Critical | 15 minutes | 2 hours |
| Priority 2 | High | 30 minutes | 4 hours |
| Priority 3 | Medium | 1 hour | 8 hours |
| Priority 4 | Low | 4 hours | 24 hours |
| Priority 5 | Cosmetic | 1 Day | 1 week |

Table 5: Priority classes

## 2.5 Define Major Incident Scenarios by Service (Scenario Routing Matrix)

With priority classes defined we can now define circumstances that will warrant an incident to be treated as a major incident. To do this a scenario routing matrix can be produced by the IT and business owners of each service. Let's use an example of an organisation that provides and supports a digital two way radio network that is a category A service:

| Scenario | Priority | Routing | Business Communication | Major Incident? | Crisis? |
|---|---|---|---|---|---|
| Catastrophic failure: Radio user are not be able to communicate via radio on all sites | Priority 1 24x7x365 | Digital Radio Support | Yes | Yes 24x7x365 | Yes CIO Level |
| Localised failure: Radio users at a single site not able to communicate via radio | Priority 2 24x7x365 | Digital Radio Support | Yes | Yes 24x7x365 | No |
| Radio users would NOT notice impact to radio environment. Services and features such as Voice recording, Client terminals, some data services and call patching will fail | Priority 3 24x7x365 | Digital Radio Support | Yes | No | No |
| Radio user would NOT notice impact to radio environment. Impact would be one of administering system | Priority 4 | Digital Radio Support | No | No | No |

Table 6: Scenario routing matrix example

This scenario routing matrix provides a service desk analyst with a simple easy to follow guide to define the priority of the incident and engage the right processes.

## 2.6  Prioritization Exceptions

As with most rules there are exceptions. Some possible exceptions are:

- Having established the rules that define what constitutes a major incident the real world can still outflank you. Where there is an incident scenario that proves to be a "grey" area it is important to define the authority to determine if it is a major incident.

- Some scenarios may be considered to be a major incident temporarily. For example if a service is continually unstable and the decision is made to provide enhanced support then additional scenarios may be temporarily constitute a major incident until stability is achieved. Another example would be where a key client is dissatisfied and at risk requiring additional scenarios impacting that client to temporarily constitute a major incident.

## 2.7 Finalise Major Incident Management Scope with the Business

Let's now summarise the agreement between the business and IT on when the major incident management process will be invoked:

- Priority classes have been defined and major incident management will be invoked when an incident is categorised as a priority 1 or priority 2 incident.
- Authorities have been defined to declare an incident as a major incident where the priority is difficult to define.
- The services that are in scope for major incident management based on their criticality are defined. "Table1: Service Categories" can be expanded to define the highest priority ticket that each category can generate:

| Service Category | A | B | C | D |
|---|---|---|---|---|
| Applicability | Vital business functions / Core shared infrastructure | Important Business functions / Vital support functions | Medium production systems | Occasional use or low priority support systems |
| Criticality | Mission Critical | Critical | Important | Low |
| Service Availability SLA | Business – 99% Infrastructure – 99.5% | 99% | 98.5% | 95% |
| Highest Possible Priority Incident | Priority 1 | Priority 2 | Priority 3 | Priority 4 |

Table 7: Finalised major incident scope

- Temporary exceptions for services or customers "in distress" can be agreed as they occur.
- Periodic reviews are agreed to ensure the service categories remain relevant.

# 3 Define Interfaces with Other Functions

Effective and efficient major incident management would require the establishment of a team with membership engaged across the organisation. When defining a major incident management process all stakeholders should be identified with responsibilities, communication channels and escalation procedures agreed. Typical stakeholders would include:

## 3.1 Service Desk

In most organisations the service desk is the single point of contact between the IT services being provided and the users. If an event has significant impact or urgency for the business/organisation it demands a response beyond the routine incident management process. When an incident is defined as a major incident normal incident management procedures are abandoned and major incident management procedures are invoked. The service desk, be it local, centralised, virtual, follow the sun or a specialised service desk group, needs to be familiar with the definition of a major incident as agreed with the business and invoke the major incident management process when appropriate. The handover process and any residual responsibilities maintained by the service desk during a major incident should be agreed and documented.

## 3.2 Business Relationship Management

Major incident management provides value to the business by resolving major incidents to minimize impact to the clients. Major incidents is highly visible to the business and is therefore relatively easy to demonstrate its value. Major incident management aligns incident resolution to real-time business priorities.

## 3.3 Crisis Management

A crisis is a major incident but with the added element of being a threat to the organisation as a whole. An example could be a catastrophic and persistent network outage impacting the entire organisations ability to function. Many corporations may have a defined crisis management process. This crisis management process should define the major incident management interface.

## 3.4 Change Management

The major incident management process will need to resolve incidents resulting from failed changes. Investigative analysis of recent changes to impacted components is typically one of the first priorities when the root cause is not known. Additionally, a change may be required to implement a workaround or resolution. This will need to be logged as a request for change (RFC) and progressed through the change management process. The process and approval authorities for emergency changes to urgently minimise the impact of a major incident should be documented.

## 3.5 IT Service Continuity Management (ITSCM)

Organisations may have a business continuity plan (BCP). Business continuity planning is the creation of a strategy through the recognition of threats and risks facing a company, with an eye to ensure that personnel and assets are protected and able to function in the event of a disaster. Business continuity management (BCM) provides initial business Impact and risk analysis activities. IT is just one service that the business relies on and IT Service Continuity Management (ITSCM) supports the BCP by producing a supporting ITSCM strategy. It supports the overall BCM process by ensuring that the required IT technical and services facilities (including computer systems, networks, applications, telecommunications, technical support and Service Desk) can be recovered within required, and agreed, business timescales For organisations where there is no BCP then ITSCM would typically perform all these activities. Figure 2 showing the overlap between incident management, major incident management and crisis management can now be extended to show the overlap between ITSCM as part of BCM.

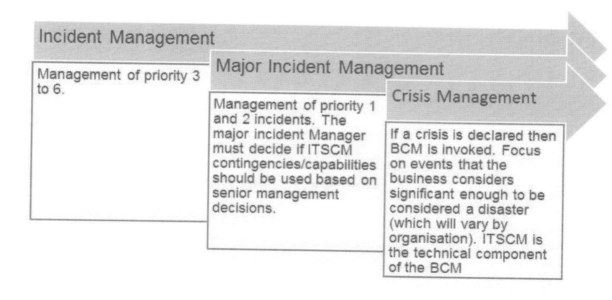

*Figure 5: ITSCM as part of BCM.*

The major incident management alignment with ITSCM and BCM needs to be clearing defined. The pre-conditions that constitute a disaster need to be defined as part of the ITSCM process. A documented strategy for recovering the IT infrastructure or IT business application after a disaster needs to be in place. Guidance will need to be provided to other areas of the business and IT on continuity and recovery related issues.

## 3.6 Resolution Management

A major incident manager relies on IT subject matter experts for technical workarounds and resolutions. These would include:

- Database administrators
- System administrators
- Application support
- Infrastructure support
- Network support
- Information security
- Access management
- Cloud, Wi-Fi, engineering and other technology resources

Resolution teams may be third party vendors. IT operations including major incident management to ensure the vendor underpinning contracts and operating level agreements are aligned with the major incident process service level agreements. The contracts should specify engagement processes and timelines. Each vendor will have unique support contracts. Some may agree join a conference line for the duration of a major incident while others will only provide high level updates published on their website. The major incident manager will need to understand the agreements with each vendor and manage stakeholder expectations accordingly.

Additionally, major incident managers will need to engage business and operations resources to manage the incident impact for its duration and after the technology incident is resolved.

Pre-defined engagement processes and communication channels should be in place with all stakeholders.

## 3.7 Service Asset and Configuration Management

The configuration management system (CMS) provides the service desk with the information required to categorised the incident and determine if the major incident management process should be invoked. It is used by the major incident manager and the resolution managers to identify faulty equipment and to assess the impact of an incident. A detailed and accurate configuration management database (CMDB) simplifies and accelerates the investigation and resolution process.

## 3.8 Capacity Management

Capacity management may develop workarounds for major incidents and help in managing any capacity issues caused by the incident.

## 3.9 Availability Management

Availability management uses incident management data to determine the availability of IT services and investigate where incident lifecycles can be improved. Expected impact on availability is a factor in defining the priority of an incident.

## 3.10 Service Level Management (SLM)

A key part of major incident management delivering to an agreed level of service is the ability to resolve incidents in a specified time. Major incident management enables SLM to define measurable responses to major service disruptions. SLM defines the required levels of service within which major incident management works. This will include:

- Major incident management engagement and response times
- Impact definitions
- Target fix times
- User and other stakeholders feedback expectations

## 3.11 Problem Management

Incident management is about restoring services as quickly as possible which may include a temporary workaround. Problem management investigates and resolves the underlying cause to prevent or reduce the impact of recurrence. The handover process should be in place for problem management to take ownership of the root cause analysis and fix implementation.

## 3.12 Defining Major Incident Management Interfaces in a Service Integration and Management (SIAM) model:

SIAM focuses on managing the delivery of services provided by multiple suppliers. SIAM is a service capability and set of practices in a model and approach that combines the benefits of best-of-breed based multi-sourcing of services with the simplicity of single sourcing, minimising the risks inherent in multi-sourced approaches and masking the supply chain complexity from the consumers of the services. SIAM assists in the situation where policy and execution can no longer be defined absolutely by a single authority, supporting the development of supply chains into supply networks.

Some SIAM models also include a centralised service desk and incident management function. Standards for exchanging incident management information must be defined. Where possible, suppliers should be encouraged to adopt your organisations major incident management standards and processes. If this is not possible SIAM will need to be competent in translating and managing multiple major incident management standards.

It is unlikely that a SIAM will get a provider of a commodity service that is used by thousands of customers worldwide to adopt its definition of incident severities. The incident management process will still need consistency by mapping the provider's severity levels to its own.

Relationships with suppliers can be the responsibility of the service level manager or owned by process owners with peer-to-peer relationships across the partner organisations. While this relationship is important, the experience is that SIAM is most effective when relationships are also built between ITIL process owner peers across the different organisations. This supports joint development of interface standards, such as common minimum incident datasets, and also supports the resolution of issues with process capability and maturity.

Challenges to be addressed when implementing a major incident management function within a SIAM model include:

- Development of common severity level definitions and what constitutes a major incident.
- Development of an effective incident management policy.
- Development of incident management toolset integration standards between suppliers.
- Development and improvement of key performance indicators.
- Development of benchmarking approaches for capability and maturity assessment and improvement. For example, where the SIAM and suppliers have different toolsets:
    - Do all parties use exactly the same severity definitions?
    - What if the SIAM uses severity 1 to 6, with 1 the highest, but the supplier uses 4 to 1 with 4 the highest?
    - What method does each provider's tool use if a 'resolved' incident isn't actually resolved?
    - Do they allow an incident to be re-opened, or does a new one have to be created?
    - Clear ownership of major incidents and problems where the causing supplier is unclear ('bouncing').

SIAM implementation must initially focus on capturing and sharing relevant incident and restoration information across all suppliers, to prevent re-occurrence irrespective of which service was initially affected. In essence, considering all suppliers to be part of the same enterprise.

# 4 Define the Engagement and Escalation Plan

What constitutes a major incident has been defined. The major incident management team participants and stakeholders have been identified and the interface with each of them defined. To ensure rapid engagement and ongoing engagement a contact list, availability roster and escalation plan by service should be defined and collated. Each of these should be available in the IT service management knowledge base with access provided to appropriate resources. These are crucial elements that will help a major incident manager quickly engage all participants as soon as possible when a major incident is declared.

## 4.1 Contact List

The contact list should capture names, job titles, telephone numbers (landline and mobile), e-mail addresses, methods of communication of various individual team members and third party suppliers involved in the major incident process. Applicable contact details should also be published in any published scenario routing matrices.

## 4.2 Availability Roster

An availability roster should be in place ensuring coverage both in and out of office hours. This roster should include coverage when key resources as out of office. An alternative is to have a single number that will forward any calls to the appropriate available resource.

## 4.3 The Escalation Plan

Escalation is a formal process to highlight the issue at hand to a higher authority. For example, if a certain team member is not willing to or is not able to do a certain activity he or she is responsible for, it is necessary to escalate the issue to the superior for resolution. A team member's questionable capability to address an issue, resource and inter-group conflicts, a major incident resolution exceeding the SLA, and a senior management decision required to invoke ITSCM are some known situations calling for escalations. These issues may require higher level intervention because the authority, decision making, resources or effort required to resolve them are beyond a major incident manager's horizon. At times, major incident manager may want to involve higher authorities for information-only escalations to keep them abreast of potential issues managing the incident.

Rules of engagement need to be defined for the major incident manager to escalate issues up the internal and third party management hierarchies when appropriate. The escalation plan provides a hierarchy of names, job titles and telephone numbers. It will contain rules guiding the major incident manager on when to invoke an escalation.

# 5 Major Incident Management Tools and Infrastructure

## 5.1 IT Service Management Software

When your information is spread over ticketing systems, emails, spreadsheets, and basic desktop management tools, management is challenging for all IT functions including major incident management. It is difficult to create end-to-end processes and you can't get the visibility you need to respond efficiently and accurately to your business. An integrated IT toolset will enable the major incident manager by providing the following:

- Incident management system with a ticketing tool that engages users and other stakeholders and can manage all processes that surround major incidents – improving visibility and control.
- Prioritizes incidents based on business impact, and drives them through the entire resolution process.
- An integrated configuration management database with relationships defined that enables evaluation of upstream and downstream impact when a specific component fails.
- Change management functionality enabling the major incident process to quickly identify and review changes applied to the impacted component(s).
- Problem management functionality enabling the association of problems with incidents.
- A knowledge base providing all supplementary information required to manage the major incident including contacts by service.
- Powerful report and performance metrics.

## 5.2 Communication Infrastructure

The ITSM software incident management ticketing system should be your primary means of communicating major incident management status to all subscribed stakeholders. In addition to e-mail SMS tools are available to establish groups to which updates can be sent or team members can be engaged. It is a good idea to have dedicated published telephone conference lines for major incidents. Collaboration tools should be in place so stakeholders can share information and work together to resolve challenging incidents.

## 5.3 War Room(s)

The MIM Plan should describe how to set up and run a "war room" for the duration of the incident. This could be a meeting room reserved for major incident management. The room could be used for other functions with the understanding that major incident management get priority as soon as a major incident is declared. It should be equipped with adequate and comfortable facilities, connectivity and PC's installed, conference phone and other phones for off line communications, flip charts, white boards, etc.

Where the stakeholders all spread across multiple locations the room is extended into a virtual war room using the available collaboration tools.

# 6 Define the Major Incident Process

Defining the sequential process, is invaluable to ensure an agreed and consistent approach to managing all major incidents.

A major incident process flow chart defines the high level process with the sequence of action to be taken for all major incidents. The following is only a simple example as each organisation will have unique processes and circumstances.

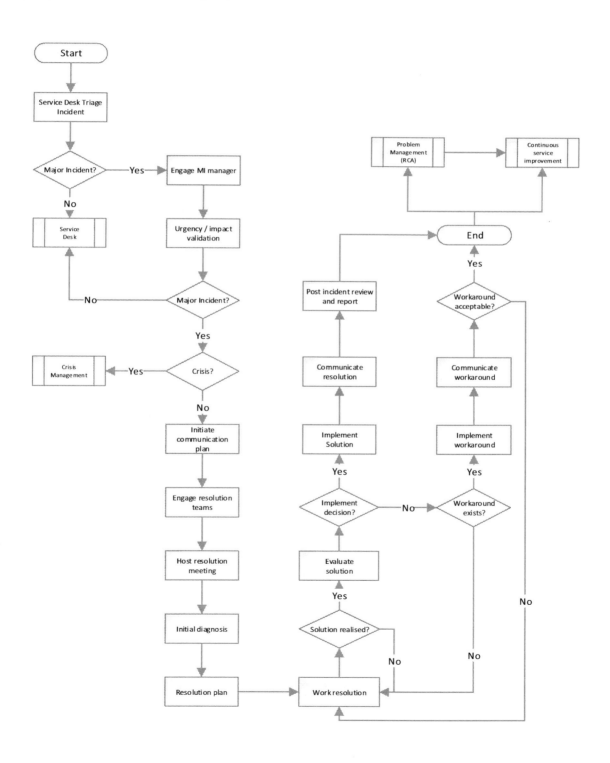

# 7   Roles and Responsibilities

Responsibilities of all major incident stakeholders need to be defined and agreed. There should be no accountability doubt or ambiguity during a major incident. One way to do this is through a RASCI matrix.

The RASCI Matrix assigns and displays responsibilities of individuals or teams during a major incident. RASCI is an acronym from the initial letters of words:

**R - Responsible** - who is responsible for carrying out the task?

**A - Accountable** - who is responsible for the task and who is responsible for what has been done?

**S - Support** - who provides support during the implementation of the activity?

**C - Consulted** - who can provide valuable advice or consultation for the task?

**I - Informed** - who should be informed about the task progress or the decisions in the task?

RASCI matrix is used for the allocation and assignment of responsibilities to the major incident team members. Use the letters R A S C I in the matrix in order to describe level of responsibility. There is a rule applied that the overall responsibility (A - Accountability) is the only one person. The people involved (R - Responsibility) should be adequate to the task. Like the flow process chart each organisation will have its unique processes. The following is a simple example:

| Activity | Service User | Service Desk | Major Incident Manager | Resolution Teams | Business |
|---|---|---|---|---|---|
| Report issue to Service Desk specifying urgency and impact | R/A | C | | | |
| Triage incident and establish priority | | R/A | | | |
| Engage the major incident manager | I | R/A | I/S | | |
| Impact / urgency validation | C | S | R/A | | |
| If appropriate engage crisis management | | | R/A | | |
| Initiate and continue the communication plan | | | R/A | S | I |
| Engage resolution teams | | | R/A | I | I |
| Join conference call / or locate to war room | I | I | R/A | R | R |
| Host technology resolution meeting | | | R/A | S | I |
| Complete initial technology diagnosis | | | R/A | R | S |
| Complete resolution plan | | | R/A | R | S/I |
| Work technology resolution | | | A | R | |
| Evaluate technology solution | | | R/A | R | C |
| Technology solution decision | | | R/A | C | I |
| Implement technology solution | | I | A | R | I |
| If required, implement technology workaround | | I | A | R | I |
| If required, implement business workaround | | I | A | I | R |
| Host post major incident review | | I | R/A | S | S |

*Figure 7: Sample RASCI chart.*

# 8  Communications Plan

Maintaining clear communications between all stakeholders is critical during a major incident. The communication plan should describe who needs to know what, how, and how often – from customers to non-involved internal staff.

The major incident manager may be accountable for executing the communication plan. In some organisations a dedicated communication manager may be responsible for communications to executives, users, clients external to the organisation and other stakeholders.

The best methods of communications vary by audience and depends primarily on three factors: rapidity of updates, number of message recipients, and confidentiality of data being shared. The following is only a simple example as each organisation will have unique processes and circumstances.

| Communication | Distribution | Frequency | Responsible | Method |
|---|---|---|---|---|
| Major incident manager engagement | Major incident manager | Once – on declaring a major incident | Service desk manager | Mobile / office / home telephone numbers |
| Updates to users reporting the issue | All users raising tickets due to the incident | Incident tickets updates at least every 30 minutes | Major incident manager | Parent incident ticket updates. Automated updates of child tickets |
| Initial resolution teams engagement | Resolution team members | Once – on declaring a major incident | Major incident manager | SMS and email includes conference line details |
| Resolution team members confirm engagement | Major incident manager | Once - With 15 minutes of receiving SMS / email | Resolution team members | Respond to SMS and/or email, Join conference call or enter war room |
| Resolution team engagement follow up | Resolution team members | Until resolution team members or their secondary are engaged | Major incident manager | Office / Home / mobile telephone numbers |
| Awareness alert IT senior management of major incident | Senior IT managers | On major incident declaration / on major incident resolution / on queries from senior management | Major incident manager | WhatsApp group |

| Communication | Distribution | Frequency | Responsible | Method |
|---|---|---|---|---|
| Updates to the impacted business community | Impacted business management | Priority 1 incident: every 39 minutes / Priority 2 incident: every 60 minutes | Major incident manager | Mass SMS group |
| Impacted external customers | Impacted external customers | Defined by the business based on the scenario | Communications Manager | Facebook / LinkedIn / company website / public address system |
| SLA breach | IT senior management, service owner, Impacted business, communications manager | On SLA breach | Major incident manager | e-mail / WhatsApp |

Figure 6: Sample communication plan template.

# 9 Post Major Incident Review

A Major Incident Review takes place after a Major Incident has occurred. The review documents the Incident's underlying causes (if known) and the complete resolution history, and identifies opportunities for improving the handling of future Major Incidents.

This is an opportunity to capture any lessons learnt, update the knowledge base and add actions to the continuous service improvement plan.

It is best practice to produce a major incident management review report within a service level agreement period of time. The following is only a simple example of a major incident review report's content as each organisation will have unique processes and circumstances.

- Short description of the incident.
- Downtime duration.
- SLA impact.
- Short incident history.
- How the incident was resolved.
- What is the root cause (if known).
- A set of activities scheduled in order to prevent this kind of downtime.

Where root cause remains unknown the problem management process is invoked to conduct the root cause analysis.

# 10 SLA's, OLA's and UC's

## 10.1 Service Level Agreement (SLA)

A service-level agreement is defined as an official commitment that prevails between a service provider and a client. For a major incident management process perspective the key SLA with the business is the maximum time to resolve an incident. Typically the higher the incidents priority the shorter the SLA period of time. The SLA may also define escalation procedures of major incidents based on the incident priority.

## 10.2 Operational-Level Agreement (OLA)

An operational-level agreement defines the interdependent relationships in support of a service-level agreement The agreement describes the responsibilities of each internal support group toward other support groups, including the process and timeframe for delivery of their services. The objective of the OLA is to present a clear, concise and measurable description of the service provider's internal support relationships. Before agreeing a major incident SLA period of time to resolve with the business it is essential that the operational-level agreements with all the major incident team members can support this SLA. For example, an SLA of 4 hours to resolve priority 1 incidents would be difficult to meet if the OLA to respond to a call out by a support group is 3 hours.

## 10.3 Underpinning Contracts (UC)

The underpinning contract is a contract between an IT service provider and a third party. The third party provides supporting services that enable the service provider to deliver a service to a customer. As is the case with OLA's the terms and conditions of underpinning contracts should reflect and be reflected in the appropriate SLAs.

# 11 Major Incident Management Metrics

It is hard to define precise and descriptive metrics for the performance of major incident management. Major incident management performance must be measured against the objective which is reiterated here:

*The purpose of the incident management process is to restore normal service operation as quickly as possible and minimize the adverse impact on business operations, ensuring that agreed levels of service quality are maintained.*

With this purpose in mind, key performance indicators (KPIs) that will help evaluate the success of major incident management could include:

- **Percentage of major incidents resolved within the agreed (SLA) time**: This KPI measures performance against a primary objective of restoring normal service operation as quickly as possible.
- **Percentage of major incidents reopened/repeated**: This KPI measures performance against the quality of the resolution be it a fix or a workaround.
- **Customer satisfaction scores**: Service owners and business representatives could score major incident management on the quality of service provided.

Managing a major incident can be stressful. A major incident manager needs to be strong, decisive, calm under pressure and authoritative enough to face senior management and customers in a hostile context. The most effective way of reducing stress while managing a major incident is preparation. To summarize the preparatory actions:

- Agree with the business what constitutes a major incident. Impacted stakeholders may encourage that the major incident management process be invoked for issues that are not necessarily major. With incidents being properly prioritised the major incident management process will not be overloaded.
- Ensure an up-to-date contact list, availability rota and escalation plan. Engaging the resolution teams and escalating when required is a crucial responsibility of a major incident manager. Without these tools progress is delayed and stress levels will rise.
- Have a structured and agreed communication plan in place. All stakeholders will know what communications they will receive and the frequency. When a major incident is declared there is momentous pressure to provide stakeholders, including customers, reliable updates.
- Have a structured and sequential major incident management process in place. This process is agreed with all stakeholders and ensures a consistent approach to managing all major incidents.
- Roles and responsibilities defined and agreed. There should be no debates around responsibilities during a major incident.

You should prepare for major incidents that continue for long durations. This includes looking after people. They will need to be fed and rosters of staff need to be put in place so they can get some rest – especially the key roles. After 12 hours under pressure, people are dangerous decision makers – including the major incident manager.

With an escalation plan in place the major incident manager needs to use it appropriately. Escalation is an increase in intensity or magnitude by bypassing the immediate person. For example, if a resolution team member is not willing to or is not able to do a certain activity, it is necessary to escalate the issue to a superior for resolution when it is not within the major incident manager's control. Escalation should be treated as a professional act and the major incident manager should not hesitate to escalate within the organisation and the third parties organisation. Major incident managers should not be reluctant to escalate for fear of the conflict it may create, potential counterattack or personal ego issues. Timely escalation by the major incident manager will ensure accountability is appropriately assigned giving superiors the opportunity to contribute to the resolution effectively.

A major incident manager does have multiple tasks to manage – team engagement, communication, escalation, team leadership and to make decisions based on all available information. Any major incident manager under pressure could attempt multitasking. This is not efficient and can be harmful to your health. You will either not fully absorb the update from the team member or the communication you are writing will not be thorough and potentially erroneous or both. You are not really multitasking, you are task-switching. Task-switching will be necessary when managing complex major incidents but the major incident manager should be aware of manage the frequency of task-switching to maximise productivity.

Lastly, people and meeting management is a skillset that any major incident needs to master. This book has focused on the hard processes that can be followed when managing a major incident. The art and science of people and meeting management is a skillset any major incident manager will require.

Printed in Great Britain
by Amazon

62811299R10021